FUGUE

LC 85-48298
ISBN 0-915306-56-5
Written by
Ivan Malinowski © 1986
Illustrated by
Dea Trier Mørch © 1986
Translated by
Carl King © 1986
Handwriting:
Ivan Malinowski
Layout : John Oreben and
Anette Heshe Nielsen
Originally published
in Danish by
Forlaget Vindrose
Denmark 1985

Distributed by
The Talman Co.
150 Fifth Ave.
N.Y., N.Y. 10011

Curbstone Press
321 Jackson Street
Willimantic
Connecticut 06226
USA

IVAN MALINOWSKI
FUGUE
ILLUSTRATED BY DEA TRIER MØRCH
TRANSLATED BY CARL KING

CURBSTONE PRESS

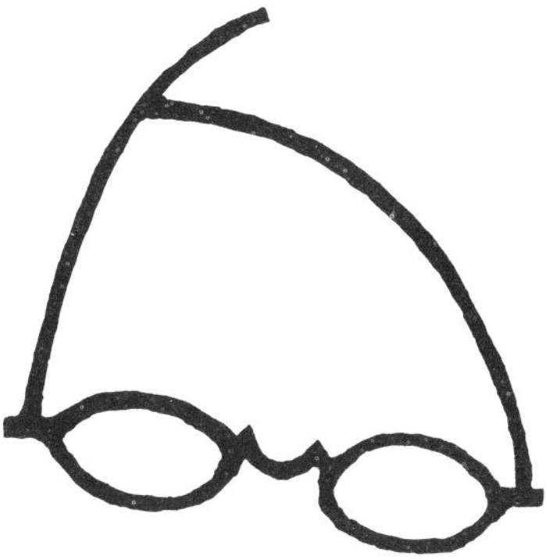

I

Full of sighs and jubilation
light and confusion
is the wind in the world.
With its mouth full
of dead peasants
and shiny tourist planes
it cries in space
above the Andes and Alps
squeaks like a mouse
in the smallest holes
and the greatest deserts
whispers in the rushes
in Hjulvhult. The wind
fills its lungs
and drowns a metropolis
in impotence and darkness

strokes the forest by its hair
the sea by its waves
drives patiently
the cunning mills
swallows an army
and spits out the grass
busily
it carries clay from Mongolia
piles thoughtless snow
on harmless Yakuts.
It stops

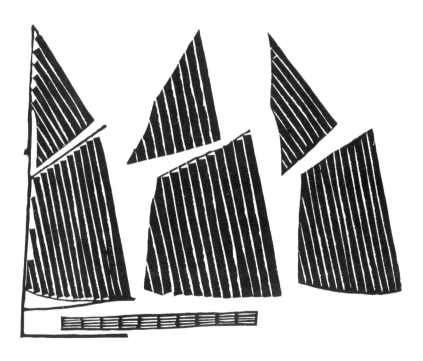

in order to gather itself
sets its spiral springs
around a centre of stillness
builds a wall
of black soil
in front of the motorist
spins the albatross
around the southern hemisphere
like a stone on a string
howls in distress at sea
falls suddenly
under Turkish stars
turns uneasily
whines in its sleep.

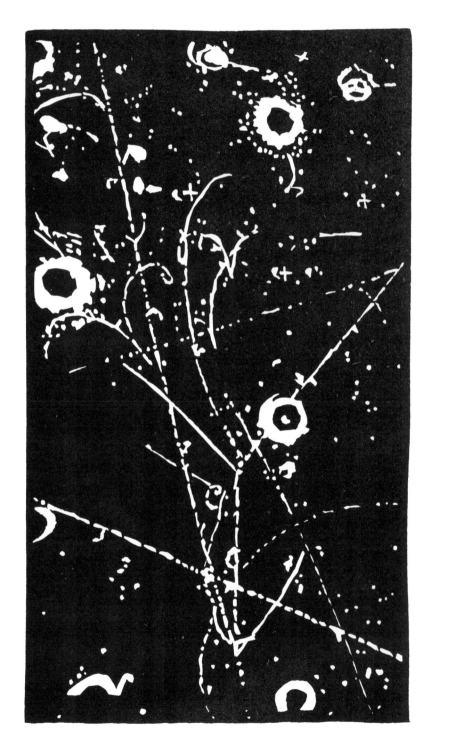

II
Restlessly roams
the wind in the world
as if it didn't believe
its own eyes.
Even though it
knows the pyramids
from personal experience
it has to finger New York
still rocking on the Li Kiang
it longs for Timbuktu
sightseeing in Soho
outside edges
among polar bears.
It does not see that everything
is everywhere
the polar bears in Brøndshøj
Timbuktu in the heart

the world in its entirety
in the smallest mote
and that travelling consequently
is pure waste of time
and energy. 'Anyone
who believes in what he sees
is a mystic' and he
has grasped a bit
of the essence of things
where he sits on his arse
while for example the wind
just flies and flies.

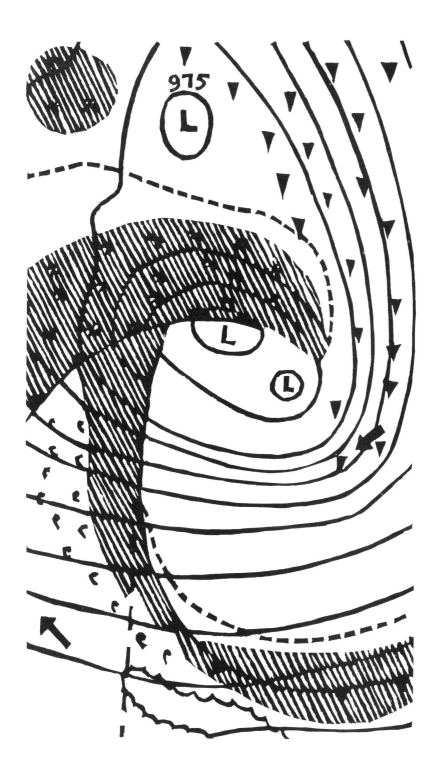

III

With its roots in its hands
it flies, hanging
in Gaia's skirts
without the least interest
in the sky or the stars.
The wind lives
unrestrained in the air
like the fish in the water's
bubble in cosmos
and the wheat in the soil's
microsphere: cells
in death's prison.
Insight is chains
free is the mouse
that gnaws on the cheese
in the trap, free
the albatross as long

as it doesn't see the string.
With its white stick
the wind knocks
at shutters and doors
and slips in under
the mud hut's threshold
and asks: was it here
I left my glasses?
Quite unable
to increase or reduce
the energy in the world
the slightest bit
it crashes like a drunken
Royal actor
in a bear skin
against Sky Mountain's
unsuspecting
coulisse, vomits
in the lap of Ophelia
belches in the barcarole
and can't even walk straight
on its own isobars.

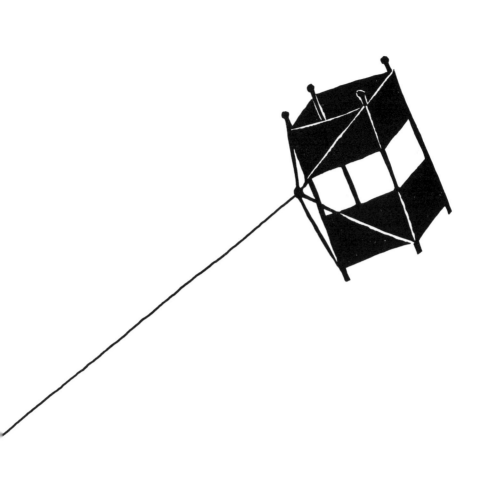

IV

But the fisherman
who from Jæren-Lista
was bound for waters
west of the Hebrides
and is already
approaching Orkney
hears of gales
from the north-east
seventeen to twenty
meters per second
snow showers and
poor visibility
and changes course
towards fifty-five
north latitude
and approximately four
east longitude

that is Dogger
which reports moderate
to falling breeze
from the north-west with showers
mainly as rain
otherwise good visibility.
Freedom is insight
in necessity.

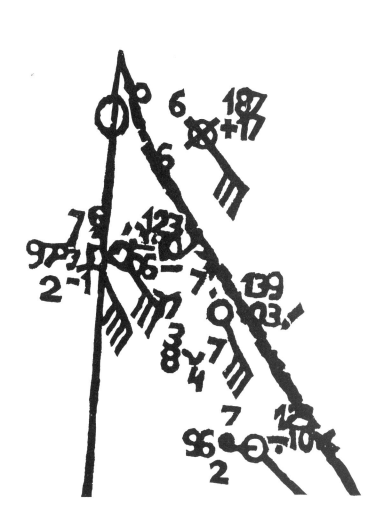

V

The Chinese Wall
stopped the attacker
by taking from him the attack's
economic basis:
his sheep and horses.
Mountain ranges brake
the lower strata of air
— the more violently
the higher howl. Kites
of sticks and paper
dance on the spot
and rise, mills
relieve the wind
that lifts the water
to the mountains' power station:
the more they toil

the more sluggishly they move
like prayer wheels
when the prayer is most fervent;
the breeze blows itself up
and ripples its muscles
but every clenched fist
conceals an outstretched hand;
the wind rose is a flower
that suspends the perception
of forwards and backwards
the dragonfly and the humming-bird
stand quietly still
in unquiet air
safer than the safest
new helicopter model
and the highland indians'
mute flutes
transmute the wind
into static ecstasy
active inactivity;
the time's and the wind's
direction and speed
do not depend
on time and wind.
The clay
is its own potter.

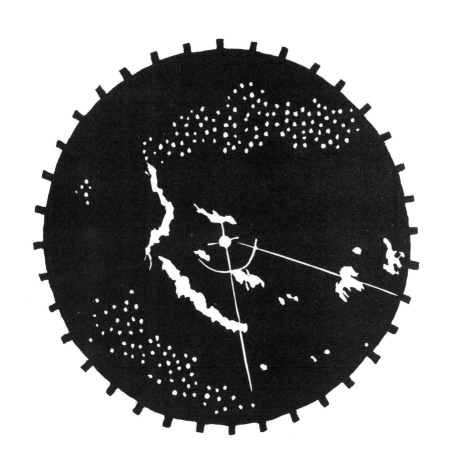

VI

Like a wolf winter runs
down through Sweden
sniffs at the carrion
scents out life.
With cartridge belt full
of mouth organs
it plays on the moors
and in the forests;
its hambo sweeps
the lakes free of snow
so the skates can sing,
the sky free of clouds
so Orion's cutting torch
can cut through
and the brain of mists.
The winter is stronger

than liquor and liberty caps
higher than havanas
and spiced better
than the best bouillabaisse
with saffron and cayenne.
As for summer
it arrives on its knees
all the way from the Ukraine
about half-past four
in a dust-grey cape
which still smells
of wormwood and
Sholokhov cocktails;
with half an eye
it sees by its quartz watch
that the birds are finished
with their mating and
swashbuckling
and for lack of better
it aids the cuckoo
with its traditional Chinese
family planning;
the summer
is a flowered cushion
for exiled heads
its sounds are supplied

by boys who blow
on empty beer bottles
while the breeze bungles
in its recitatives
and confuses the variations:
its score has flown off the stand
and flutters like white bats
above the evening meadows.
March and September
are two rusty hinges
where the year hangs
cries in pain
slams in the wind.

VII

'Lions are we all
but lions on a flag;
when they move
and start to attack
it is the wind which kindly
gives them life; their assault
is formidable
and fully visible
whereas the wind
is not to be seen at all.
May that which is not seen
not be withheld us!'
The bricklayer when you sleep
in the house he built;
the cow's and the grape's
trustful eyes

when you eat and drink;
the poet and the dreamer
when you think and sing
or just listen to the radio;
the pistons and pinions,
Citroën's Algerian
worker and the desert's
oil and sweat
when at a hundred and ten
kilometers an hour
you drive through your country
and feel like a lion!
God is a web
incapable
of catching a fly
a ghost who doesn't
move a mote
or fill a flag.
Remember the motors
to keep them holy:
the day labourer, grey
from the dust with which he toils
the winegrower
glowing red
like his own soil
and the freezing fisherman

almost ocean-blue
in the mug: they are all
so difficult to perceive! But
'may that which is not seen
not be withheld us!'

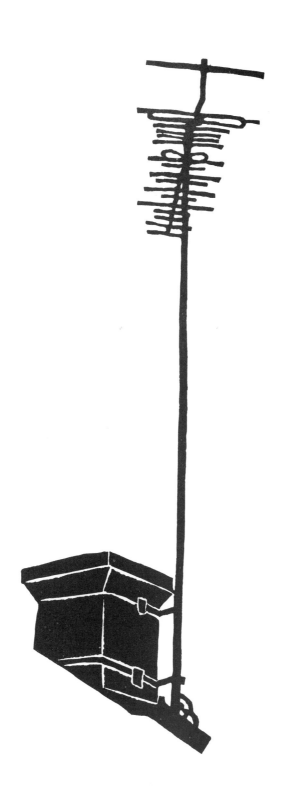

VIII

A strong storm centre
attracts air masses
in the form of wind
from all sides simultaneously
so the migrating Canadian
Tennessee warbler
unexpectedly may meet
the Lena river's little
yellow-browed warbler
in Thorshavn where William
sits in his cellar
and listens to the wind
like the bow to the string:
whether it really
after the introduction's
disguised two-part harmony

can set the tone
as if out of thin air
and shape the next
sixteen bars
as a long legato
led to half close.
Fermata. Pause.
Then something happens:
an Indian called
Rykardo lands
bewildered in Tokyo
while his letter box
left behind in the calm belt
is attacked by the trade wind
and my letters from Denmark
in bad Spanish.

The simoom bombards
the Tuaregs' Tamanrasset
with sand from Mali
so the eyes over the veils
can't see a hand in front of them
the drums sound
half-smothered at night
and two tourists
are cut off
from the world
while all the while
the Trans-Siberian
with shining bikes
and crocheted antimacassars
rolls like a millipede
through the taiga's growing
snowfall from the east.
Like a good worker
the wind works:

with the available,
transforms tirelessly
tests all
possibilities imaginable
spares even the unthinkable
a thought:
seed from Sri Lanka
—such as coconuts—
sprouts in Somalia
and Turkes in Tåstrup;
fortunes are gathered
in drifts and scattered
again over the world
by those resolute
watersprouts which go
by the name of revolutions;
evidence proves
that cotton was sailed
across the Pacific
from Asia before Columbus

stumbled upon America;
the preaching priest
is borne by his gas balloon
to the seventh heaven,
the mulatto on the wrecked
Medusa's life raft
makes landfall of Livo
and I in Hjulbhult
am in reality in the West Indies.
So don't say that the wind
doesn't know what it's doing
or do what it can.

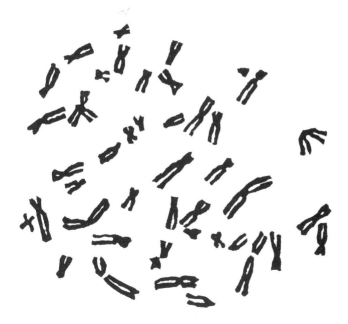

IX

In the snow drift on Rügen
the cranes await
impatiently in March
a favourable wind
to be carried over the sea
dance their dances
and populate at last
Scandinavia's
empty heaths
fields and moors
with new dancers
and spring trumpets.
What friendly wind
brought you here
from Central European
turbulences
and let you address me

with your namesake
the Moabite's words:
'Whither thou goest
I will go
and where thou lodgest
I will lodge
thy people shall be my people
and where thou diest
will I die and there
will I be buried'
well aware
that also my country
exists only on the map
that also my people
in misery
are scattered over the world
so we must beseech the wind
to be able to visit them;
well aware
that your initials
and mine
don't grow in any
tree's bark
confined in a heart;
well aware

that your grave and mine
will never be marked
with cross or star
or weighed down by stone
but only be found
in the wind.

X

'Here I come
The Wrath of the Plains
Isaiah and Jeremiah
in one person,
The Light Bringer
When Night is Deepest,
Quencher of Thirst
– innumerable like my acts
are my _noms de guerre_.
I upset or erect you
according to circumstances. Soft
I blow on the hard,
hard games I play
with the soft. I
was the boy Odysseus'
playmate, wasn't I ?

Without dwelling place
I raze dwelling places
to the ground.
It is me who bellows
in Bach's passions
wails in the Jews'
kaddishim, sobs
in the gypsies' saetas.
I laugh and cry
in all tongues
even Tabassaran
with 52 cases,

fuck in Danish
the sexless,
am quiet in none.
Without accent
I told Stalin
home truths in Georgian,
no Hitler or Banzer
gags me,
in Kurdish I spit
Evren in the face!
I box the ears
of the Upper Ones,
my gusts are no respecters
of persons,
my reach is exceeded
only by my unreachability,
I am supreme
within my sphere,
I, the wind
Superman'

$E = mc^2$

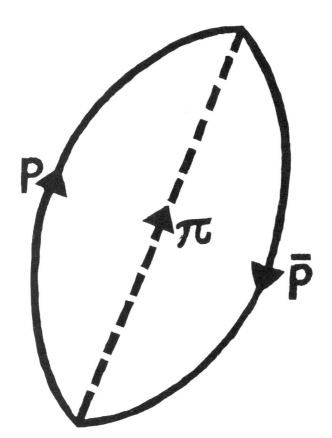

XI

There is draught in the world:
matter is leaky
and energy clotted
the eternal mountains
are aquariums which teem
with agile perishable
components and
components' components
which whirl around each other
in imperishable
ingenious patterns
and at great speed.
Of all the world's endless
myriads of particles
there can only be one
that stands still

and that moves furiously
like a swarm of bees.
Incessantly the indivisible
divides itself
voluntarily and seemingly
with pleasure.
Stability
– stone or state –
is apparent:
the set surfaces
are temporary masks
of indomitable forces;
more mobile than music
peoples and classes
constantly change place;
where the Picts lived
live pale lords,

on the princes' steps
lie flower children,
revolt upon revolt
walks against the wind
and turns it,
stubborn structures
go through history
and defy meteorology:

the genetic code
tacks death
like the sail enables you
with the aid of the wind
to travel against the wind.
They who 'build the future'
try to build
a prison for the river
that runs. 'The certain
is not certain, nothing
remains as it is'
Granite crumbles
and skyscrapers
of reinforced concrete
and world dominion
and ideologies.
The best building site
is movement.

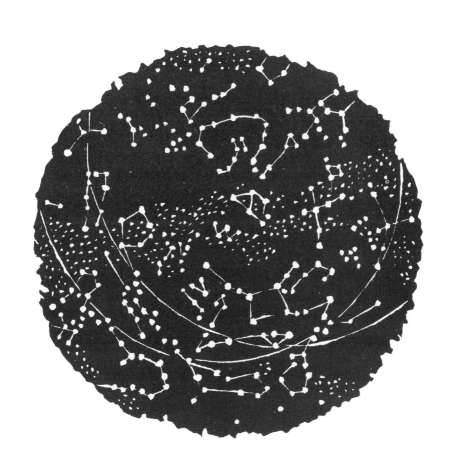

XII

What doesn't the wind
touch on?
As foehn or bora
it rolls down the mountains
with its cold letters
lands with a smack
on the tiled floor
of the gay bar
mumbles awkwardly
'a beer, from the crate, please'
It howls in the towns'
black gates
sample-smells
disguised as sirocco
the Chinese grill's
tortured deep-fry
the toilets' bouquet

of tar and urine;
in the mistral's correct
Prussian uniform
Made in England
it times the riviera's
snarling nightingales
is present
as a tacit hurricane
in the most evil-smelling
editorial offices.
As monsoon it has the best
basis for understanding
weathercocks and windbags:
the reddest banners
blow with the wind.
Originally salted
by Jensen the Jute
today it delivers
festering clouds
franked with French
and German stamps
or cleans at once now
the air in Holmbladsgade
when it chooses.
Without passport or visa

compass or return ticket
it moves without permission
like an army across a plain
or in the form of a column
or in jerks or coils
round and round
and where it has been
nothing is the same:
smouldering ruins

mutilated bodies
and sand sculptures.
Its masculine ballets
and heroic operas
with clashing swords
and crashing suits of armour
raise the dust
and attract attention.
Does nothing happen
on calm sea? In dead calm?
The arctic tern knows better
and the hoopoe
and you sister.

XIII

Does the wind know
the way? Does the clock know
what time it is?
What does ornithology
mean to birds?
Is the snail on the gravestone
reading a date?
Why does it grow dark
mum? Does
the centre never shift?
Can it hold?
Can't the breeze
spell calm?
Does the computer also remember
that it comes from China
via Leibniz and the Jesuits?

Is the sun aware of
what a complicated course
it runs around me
Ivan Malinowski
not least when I move?

On what conditions
does the rain condescend?
Can you describe a horse
by saying what it does not
look like?
What is the opposite
of the speed of light?
Does the pursued
in reality pursue his pursuer?
Why are there so many
sprinters? Swifts?
Missiles? Machines?
Can you keep the sun

in the dark?
What do you call the wind
when it's not blowing?
The express when it sleeps
in its shed? The revolution
when it has succeeded?
How is one hand
able to overtake the other
on the keys without moving?
Doesn't the speedometer move
when it shows zero?

Do the stars still not know
one another
after all these years?
What about us?
Why fly in the air
in a Concorde
when the goal is a hole
in the ground? Does the air
feel the birds?
Will the wind remember
the grass and us?

Hjulvhult 31/12 84 - 20/4 85
Galargues 24/6 - 11/7 85

Notes

I _Hjulshult_ — place in Sweden where the poet lives when not in Denmark or elsewhere

Yakuts — people in N.E. Siberia

II _Brønshøj_ — lower middle-class suburb of Copenhagen

III _Gaia_ — Greek goddess personifying earth, 'Mother Earth'

Sky Mountain — 'Himmelbjerget', one of the highest points in Denmark (147 metres!)

the soil's microsphere — the average thickness of soil is 25 centimetres

barcarole — 'boat song', swaying, romantic melody

<u>isobars</u> – lines on a chart connecting places having the same barometric pressure. The wind blows mainly along the isobars. The front cover illustration depicts an isobar chart

IV <u>Jæren-Lista</u> – localities in Southern Norway, often mentioned on the radio shipping forecast

<u>Dogger</u> – sandbank in the North Sea between England and Denmark, famous fishing ground

VI <u>hambo</u> – Swedish folk dance

<u>liberty cap</u> – Psilocybe semilanceata, small, quite common mushroom, which is a strong euphoriant

<u>Sholokhov cocktails</u> – Georgian cognac mixed with Crimean champagne instead of mineral water

VIII <u>Thorshavn</u> – capital of the Faroe Islands in the North Atlantic

William – William Heinesen, famous Faroese writer, born 1900

fermata – a symbol that indicates that a note or beat is to be held longer than usual

simoom – a hot, dry, dust-laden desert wind

Tuareg – nomadic Berber people of Africa

Tamanrasset – oasis in the Southern Sahara

antimacassar – a covering to protect the back of a chair or seat from brilliantine. Macassar: Indonesian town which produces hair-dressing

Tåstrup – a Copenhagen suburb

Livø – a tiny Danish island

IX **Rügen** – an island off the coast of Northern Germany, last stop for many Scandinavian migratory birds

X **nom de guerre** – 'war name', pseudonym

kaddishim – plural of kaddish, Jewish prayer for the dead

saeta – religious Andalusian gypsy song

Tabassaran – East Caucasian language

Danish, the sexless – The Danish language has two genders. They are called 'neuter' and 'common' gender

Banzer – Bolivian landowner and former dictator

Evren, Kenan – Turkish general, the real ruler since the coup in 1980. Oppressor of millions of Kurds, their language and culture, in Turkey

XI _the indivisible_ – the word atom comes from the Greek 'atomos', indivisible. The illustration opposite part II shows neutrinos – subnuclear particles of 0 rest mass – registered in a so-called 'bubble chamber'

Picts – Scotland's aboriginal Celtic population. From the latin

- picti meaning 'painted', 'co=
loured'

XII foehn, bora, sirocco, mistral -
different winds

  Jensen the Jute - Johannes V.
Jensen, Danish writer, 1873-1950,
Nobel Prize for Literature 1944

  Holmbladsgade - heavily
polluted street in Copenhagen,
with a high rate of cancer

XIII Ivan Malinowski - Danish
poet, born 1926. Works in Eng=
lish: 'Critique of Silence' (Se=
lected poems.) Curbstone Press
1977

The poem contains quotes
from Tuomas Anhava, Karl
Marx, Jalal al-Din Rumi,
Pablo Neruda, The Bible, Ber=
tolt Brecht, Bo Rasmussen and
Octavio Paz